The Elementary Entrepreneur

Julian Alfaro

Table of Contents

Introduction 1

Chapter 1: Confidence 6

Chapter 2: Find Your Obsession 16

Chapter 3: Don't Quit 25

Chapter 4: Find Mentors 31

Chapter 5: Learn How to Sell 40

Chapter 6: If You Aren't Learning You Aren't Succeeding 47

Chapter 7: Take Action Now 55

Chapter 8: Create Your Own Future 60

Introduction

My name is Julian Alfaro. I am 8 years old, and I am an elementary entrepreneur. You may wonder what that is. Well, I'm glad you asked because I'm going to tell you. An elementary entrepreneur is a kid that wants to become an entrepreneur, so he takes all of these really difficult ideas and makes them as simple as possible so even a kid can do it.

At a very young age, my dad had me start watching motivational videos. Even though it may sound strange to some people, my dad wanted me to start learning about success before I became an adult. So, you may be thinking, what does an 8-year-old know about success? The answer is, a lot!

You see, so many people wait until they are an adult to start thinking about their goals, dreams, and future. They think that kids are just supposed to play and have fun. They can worry about their future later. While this may be true for some kids, that is not how I want to spend my childhood. There are so many kids around the world today that are doing some really huge things to impact the world and become successful.

Introduction

Open up YouTube right now and you will see so many videos made by kids that have millions of views. Kids are starting businesses, inventing things, helping people in need, and training for the Olympics. They are the kids that decided they didn't want to just be average. They didn't just want to be a kid. They had big dreams and took massive action to achieve them.

I am one of these kids. I don't just want to spend my childhood playing video games and running around outside. While I still do those things, and I believe that relaxing is important, I also have big goals I want to accomplish. I don't just want to be another average kid that becomes an average adult who makes an average impact. I want to be a savage kid that becomes a savage adult who changes the world.

I know that I'm not the only kid out there that feels this way. So, I'm writing my book to that kid. The one that really wants to do something great with their life, but they don't know where to start. The one that has big goals but doesn't have any confidence. The one that is different and gets bullied at school. I'm writing to you.

In this book, I'm going to tell you what I learned about success through my mentors, books, podcasts, live events, and YouTube videos. As you read, I want you to take notes. Share what you are learning with your parents and your friends. Connect with me on social media @thelementaryentrepreneur so we can chat.

Remember, this book will only help you if you want to become a savage kid. If you are comfortable being average, then this book is not for you. Get ready to have fun and be challenged to become better than you were before.

Are you ready? Let's go!

Chapter 1
Confidence

I'm putting this chapter first because I believe it is one of the most important skills that you need to have if you want to become successful. In fact, this used to be my biggest struggle. I hated to look at people in the eye and talk to other people, especially adults. The funny part is that I didn't have any problems talking at home. I was very confident when it came to talking to my parents and siblings. The problem came when I left the house.

My dad noticed that this was a struggle for me, so he decided to help me overcome my nervousness. Guess what he made me do? Go door to door and sell success postcards. These postcards had inspirational quotes on them, and it was my job to introduce myself to the person who opened the door and try to sell them the cards. Crazy, right? That's exactly what I thought!

I really didn't want to do this. I begged my dad to not make me do it, but he told me that the more I did it, the easier it would become. Since I trust my dad and listen to what he says, I made myself do it. So, with a stack of postcards in my hand, I started walking down the street in my neighborhood. My dad was walking with me. When I turned to walk up to the first door, I was so scared. My palms were sweating, my face was on fire, and my heart was beating so hard, it sounded like a drum.

My dad gave me a pat on the back and said, "You can do it, buddy." I knocked on the door quietly, and I was secretly hoping that no one answered the door. Unfortunately, the door swung open and an older lady stood in the doorway. With a huge smile on my face and without even thinking, I started my sales pitch that I memorized. "Hi, my name is Julian Alfaro! Do you want to buy a postcard?"

I know this is not the best sales pitch, but it was the best I could do. I wanted to hurry up and get out of there. Shockingly, the lady asked me questions about the cards such as, what are they, who are they for, and how much are they? The more I talked to her, the calmer I became. My hands weren't sweating anymore, my heart was back to its normal pounding sound, and my face turned back to its regular color.

The lady ended up buying one card, which made me really happy. Even though it was a small sale and I didn't do great with my pitch, I was still able to sell! After I left the first house, I wish I could say that I was no longer nervous and filled with confidence. The truth is that I was still scared. But the best part is, after every house, it started becoming easier. My pitch even got better, and I was able to talk more with people I didn't know.

After we finished for the day, I looked at my dad and said, "Dad, that was actually pretty fun. Are we going to do it again?" My dad said that we were going to be doing it a few times a week to help me build my confidence even more. Instead of being scared, I was actually pretty excited.

I don't want to say that I've mastered confidence, but I have become so much more confident. As with any skill, it is something I'm always trying to get better at. To help you, I'm going to give you some tips to help you become more confident.

1. Positive Words - The first step in building your confidence is to believe in yourself. It doesn't matter who believes in you; if you don't believe in yourself, you will never become confident. You have to be your biggest and loudest cheerleader.

This means that you should never say words like, "I can't do it," "I'm not good enough," "I will never be able to do it," "I am shy." Every single day, you need to say words like, "I can do it," "I am smart," "I can achieve my goals," "I am confident.'

I want you to make a list of positive words that you can say about yourself. Write down at least 5 things. Each morning before school and each evening before you go to bed, I want you to say those words out loud. Stand in front of a mirror, look at yourself, and say those words with a smile. Don't just mumble the words. Say them loud like you are yelling for your favorite team to score the winning goal.

2. Make eye contact - I used to think that one of the most awkward parts of speaking with people I didn't know was making eye contact. I used to

talk to people with my eyes facing the floor. The minute I would look up, I would feel so stupid, so I would look back at the floor.

The best way to get better at making eye contact is to practice. When you meet new people, shake their hand and introduce yourself. Say, "Hello, my name is Julian Alfaro." While you are introducing yourself, make eye contact with them. Ask for their name and when they start talking, keep making eye contact. You don't have to have a long conversation but try doing this with people you don't know. This will help you practice making eye contact without feeling like you have to talk to them for a long time.

3. Ask Questions - Asking questions is a great way to build your confidence because it helps you become more comfortable when talking with other people, especially people you don't know. Being able to talk to other people without feeling shy or nervous is an important part of having confidence. You can start practicing this when you go to the store or go out to eat. Try to ask the waiter or cashier 3 questions. You can ask 1. What is your name? 2. Where are you from? 3. What do you like to do for fun?

Having confidence is so important, so I hope that you try to use these three tips to build your confidence. If you want to do better at school, make more friends, stand out in a crowd, and become more successful, you must be confident. It is my goal to become one of the most confident kids on the planet, so I'm trying to practice as much as I can. I hope that you do the same.

Chapter 2
Find Your Obsession

Neymar da Silva Santos is one of the world's most famous soccer players. He has won many awards and championships, and in 2016, ESPN said that he was the fourth most famous athlete. When he was very young, Neymar knew that he wanted to become a soccer player. Also, his father used to play professional soccer. This meant that Neymar practiced soccer every chance he got. He became obsessed with it. The definition of obsession is to become controlled by a powerful force or strong emotion.

His father gave him a practice schedule, and everyday Neymar would go over his soccer drills, run, and watch soccer games to learn new skills. Because he was so good, professional scouts started paying attention to him. At 11 years old, he started training with professional soccer clubs. When he was 17, he signed his first contract to play with a professional soccer team. Ten years later, Neymar is still winning championships and earning millions of dollars doing what he loves.

The reason that Neymar became so successful at a young age is that he found his obsession, and he worked at it. Everyday, he practiced for hours. Even now, he spends about 5 hours per day practicing. His obsession was connected to something that he loves to do. Neymar once said, "I'm always happy when I play. When you're happy, things naturally work out; when you're sad, things never work out."

This is one of the reasons that I think Neymar is the greatest. He found his obsession and went after it. In fact, Neymar is the one that inspired me to fall in love with soccer. I've been playing soccer for as long as I can remember, and I love it. Everyday, I practice my foot work with my friends, I watch soccer games, and I play on a soccer team.

When I'm playing soccer, it doesn't feel like I'm working. Like Neymar said, I feel happy while I'm doing it.

Now, I have a question to ask you. What is your obsession? What makes you happy? The answers to these questions are important because everyone needs an obsession. Everyone needs to have something that they love to do. The reason for this is that your obsession is the thing that is going to make you a lot of money.

Instead of looking for a job that may not pay you a lot of money and make you unhappy, seek to find an obsession. A job may be a place that you go and do work that you hate to do. That is a sad life. An obsession allows you to do something that you love to do, makes you happy, and brings you money.

We all need to have an obsession, and to help you find yours, follow these steps.

1. Find Out What You Like - What is something that you like to do? What can you stay up all night working on? Now, your answers have to be something other than playing video games or watching movies. That is entertainment. Think about other things that you like to do. Do you like to cook? Do you like to make crafts? Are you good at sports? Do you like to make

YouTube videos? Figure out what you like to do most.

Start by making a list of the things that you really like to do. From that list, pick the top three. Then, from those three, choose the number one thing that you really like to do. More than likely, this is going to be your obsession. This is the thing that you are going to spend most of your time working at so that you can become better.

2. Start Working - I don't want you to think of work as a negative word. It is actually a really great word. Once you find your passion, you must put the work in. Another obsession I have

is becoming a YouTuber. I really like making small videos for kids that help motivate and inspire them. It's not enough for me to just like doing it. I have to prepare what I'm going to say, film it, edit it, and then post it. I also have to watch other YouTubers to get ideas and inspiration for how to improve my videos.

Once you find your obsession, you must put in work EVERY SINGLE DAY. Whatever your obsession is, try to become a little better every day. One of the best ways to do this is by learning. Read books, watch videos, listen to podcasts, and get a mentor. All of these tools will help you learn more about your obsession and become better. If you want to play basketball, watch professional basketball games and study the moves of the best players in the game. Read books about basketball. Listen to podcasts about basketball. You get the idea.

3. Learn from Your Mistakes - The word, "fail" is not a bad word. If you are going to become better at something, you are going to fail. When I'm playing in a soccer game, there are many times that I've tried to score a goal and miss. I can do 2 things after missing the goal. I can become upset with myself and give up, or I can

figure out why I missed the shot and practice to get better at my skills.

As you are working on your obsession, there are going to be times that you are going to fail. You may not do really great, but that is ok. You have to start somewhere. The first time you try, you may not succeed. In fact, you may have to try 10 times before you get better. But NEVER give up. Keep failing, keep trying, and keep learning.

Chapter 3
Don't Quit

In the book, *Think and Grow Rich*, by Napoleon Hill, he tells a story about a guy named R.U. Harby. Harby's uncle wanted him to help him dig for gold. They started digging and found a little bit of gold. They both got really excited and decided to buy heavy equipment to dig deeper. They dug for a long time, but only got a little more gold. After a while, they got discouraged and decided to quit. They sold their digging equipment to a garbage man for a couple hundred dollars and went back home.

The garbage man decided to hire a mining expert who told him that if he dug three more feet, he would hit gold. The garbage man took the equipment and dug three feet and found more gold than he knew what to do with. He was now a very rich man.

R.U. Harby and his uncle missed out on that huge amount of gold because they quit. And here is the crazy part. They were only THREE FEET away from the gold! THREE FEET!

Can you imagine how upset you would be if you missed out on becoming rich by just three feet? Well, this is what can happen if we quit. Like I talked about in the last chapter, failure can make us quit. The problem with that is we could have been close to something really great if we had just kept going.

Quitting should never be an option. When you are working hard, keep working even if you don't see immediate success. For example, I post YouTube videos a lot. My videos don't have that many views. I can quit because my number of views is too low to me. But, if I quit, then I'll never be able to make the viral video that I know I'm going to make. Even the greats had to start somewhere.

Caleb Maddix, my mentor, tells a story about doing Periscope videos. When he first started, he would only get a few viewers. Even though he got a little discouraged, he didn't quit. One day, he didn't even want to do a video, but he made himself do it. There were only 3 people watching the video that day, which upset him. But, one of those people was Grant Cardone's sister. If you don't know Grant Cardone, he is one of the most successful entrepreneurs alive.

Anyways, Grant's sister told him that he needed to get Caleb Maddix on his show. A short time later, Caleb was able to be on Grant Cardone's show that was watched by thousands of people. He was able to do this because he didn't quit with his videos.

If Caleb had been like R.U. Harby and quit because he was disappointed, he may not have had the chance to meet Grant Cardone. What might you be missing out on because you keep quitting? You may be close to a big breakthrough, but you keep quitting.

My message to you is, "STOP!" Stop quitting! If you are not doing well in Math class, never stop trying to study and learn. If you are working on your free throw, never stop trying to make it into the basket. If you are learning how to cook but you keep burning your food, never stop trying to make the best meal ever tasted.

Don't quit until you reach the gold. Even if people don't think you will be able to achieve your dreams. Keep working hard. I'm sure people didn't think much of the garbage man but look at what he was able to do. While everyone else quit, he decided to give it another shot. He became rich because of it. Never say, "I quit?" say, "I will keep going until I win!"

Chapter 4
Find Mentors

Everybody needs to have a mentor. You may be wondering, what is a mentor? A mentor is a wise and trusted teacher. They help you become better and guide you towards success. Let me tell you a story about a kid named, Samuel. When Samuel was in Kindergarten, he did not do well in school at all. He got into fights with other kids, was disrespectful to his teachers, and wouldn't do any of his schoolwork. It was clear that he needed some help. He didn't know his dad and his mom had a drug problem. Without a mentor in his life, Samuel was going to have a difficult life ahead of him.

When Samuel went into the first grade, a mentor came into his life. An older man took the time to talk to, train, and guide Samuel. In less than a year, Samuel's grades, behavior, and relationships got better. Mentors are so powerful because they are like a partner that gives you extra support.

When I was younger, my dad had me read books, watch videos, and listen to podcasts and audiobooks by very successful entrepreneurs. He still has me do this. Because of this, I was able to learn so much from them, and it has helped me write down my goals, work harder, and chase my dreams.

The best part is that I've been able to meet some of these successful people, and one of them has become my personal mentor and best friend, Caleb Maddix. If you don't know who he is, then you have to look him up. He is 16 years old, and he is a very successful entrepreneur and speaker. He has helped me so much and continues to give me tips to become better.

Some of the other mentors that I've met are Russell Brunson, Tony Robbins, and Grant Cardone. I have studied their material and met some of them in person, which has really helped me. If you don't have a mentor, then you must get one. I'm going to tell you about the three types of mentors that you can have that will change your life.

1. Your Parents or Trusted Adult - I know some of you may be confused by this, but your parents are the first mentors that you have in your life. For me, my dad and mom have been really important in my life. They teach me and guide me in the right direction. My dad is always giving me pointers and helping me get better at soccer, with school, and with becoming an entrepreneur.

It is very important that you realize that even if your parent annoy you sometimes, you must still respect them as your mentors. They know what they are talking about. They have been through a lot in life and can give you great advice to help you become successful. Don't ignore what they say. Listen to what they say and follow it. That's the most important part about having a mentor. You must listen to what they say and then actually do it.

2. Personal Mentor - Remember when we talked about your obsession? Well, whatever your obsession is, find someone that is an expert at it. Once you find that person, try to get in contact

with them. Message them on social media, comment on their posts, or email them. Whatever you need to do, try to contact them. Ask them questions about what they did to get to where they are. You want to find someone that has achieved what you want to achieve.

For example, I want to become an entrepreneur, so my dad showed me one of Caleb Maddix's videos. After watching it, I knew that I wanted to meet Caleb. This led me to trying to contact him. A short time later, I was able to meet him. If you are persistent, you will be able to meet your mentor in person and be able to ask them important questions.

3. **Distant Mentors** - Distant mentors are experts that you are unable to meet in person. They are people that you can find online, in books, on podcasts, or on videos. I have many mentors that I have not met in person. They mentor me through their material. Even though I've never met Napoleon Hill (he is dead), I still consider him one of my mentors because I've listened to his book many times.

Find as many distant mentors as you can. Their material may be all over the Internet and in bookstores. Study all of it. Learn as much as you can from experts that you may not be able to sit down and talk to, but you can learn just as much information from studying their material. If you want to be a singer, then you should be studying all of Beyonce's videos. Read as much as you can about her career and what she did to achieve her success. If you want to become a chef, watch Gordon Ramsey's shows, read his book, and study his career.

You will be able to achieve so much more with great mentors in your life. Make a list of people that can be your personal mentors and distant mentors. Also, have a conversation with your parents or a trusted adult about wanting them to become your mentors. Think of it like picking people to be on your team. If you are the captain of your team and you want to win, you are going to pick the best players to help your team win. The same is true for mentors. You want the best mentors on your team so you can win.

Chapter 5
Learn How to Sell

As an elementary entrepreneur, selling is one of the most important things to learn because it is the only way to build a business. I mentioned earlier that my dad took me door to door selling. The first time I did it, I made $85 selling success post cards. Selling is one of the quickest ways to make money as a kid. If you have a product, you should be selling it so that you can build your business.

One benefit of selling is you have the potential to make a lot of money. For example, I bought a box of candy from a wholesale store. I went door to door and sold the complete box of candy in a little over an hour. I made $50 profit in that short amount of time. I'm going to give you some tips to help you start selling today.

1. Believe in Yourself - We talked about this in the confidence chapter, but it is so important that I wanted to say it again. You have to believe that you are a great salesperson. If you lack confidence, you will not be able to sell. Speak positive affirmations before you sell your product, and the person you are selling to will

feel your confidence. They will want to buy your product because they know that you believe in yourself and your product.

2. Focus on the Value of the Product - First of all, don't sell anything that you don't believe in. If you don't like what you are selling, you are going to have a hard time selling it. Believe in the product that you are selling and focus on its value.

I remember when I was selling the postcards and people would say that it was too much money. Instead of walking away from the sale, I would focus on the value of the product. Even though they felt like it was too much money, I let them know that their money was going to be given to something that is valuable and will make their lives better.

3. Enthusiasm - You MUST be excited about selling. If you try to sell something to someone and you seem sad or depressed, they will not want to buy from you. However, if you have a big smile on your face, your voice is loud and confident, and you are making eye contact, they will sense your enthusiasm. This type of attitude will make more people want to buy your product.

4. Practice - If you master the action, you will master the success. The more you sell, the

better you will become. Don't get discouraged if you only make $5 on your first day of selling. Save that $5 and go out the next day and try to make $10. Always be selling, and it will become a habit. It will be like riding a bike.

The first time you rode a bike, you probably fell a couple times and the bike wobbled. You didn't feel comfortable. But, after riding it a few times, it became easier until you didn't even have to think about it. The same is true with sales. The more you do it, the easier it will become.

5. Good Manners - Always say, "Yes, sir," and "Yes, ma'am." You should always be using manners, but it is even more important when

you are selling. You are asking someone for something of value, which is their money. They work hard for their money, so you should be respectful when you are selling to someone. Talk to them respectfully and with kindness.

6. Have a Positive Attitude – Attitude is everything in selling, communicating, and in life. You need to have an, "I can do it," "I will get it done," and a "No problem" attitude. Have a positive attitude will get you more results at home, in school, in business, and everywhere you go.

If you start putting these tips into action, you will become a selling machine. For all the money you make, put it aside and start saving it. Use the money to invest in your business or your obsession. Don't just waste your money on video games or candy. Use your money to make you more successful in your future.

Chapter 6
If You Aren't Learning You Aren't Succeeding

When I was 4 years old, my dad got me a comic book called, *Escape the Rat Race*, by Robert Kiyosaki. It was a book about money. I loved this book. It was what got me interested in saving and earning money. From that point forward, my dad had me listen to books. That's right. That's my secret. Before I could even read, my dad had me listen to audiobooks and watch YouTube videos of Tony Robbins, Tim Storey, Darren Hardy, and many more. He did this because he understood the value of learning.

Robert Kiyosaki says, "When you're young, work to learn not to earn. That means that instead of trying to get money, try to get the knowledge that will eventually pay you a lot of money.

Caleb Maddix told a story about how his dad did not pay him to do chores. Instead, his dad paid him $20 for every success book he read. My dad loved this idea so much that he started paying me to read success books as well. Some of the books I've read are:

1. *Success Principles* by Jack Canfield

2. *10X Rules* by Grant Cardone

3. *Positive Dog* by Jon Gordon

4. *Rich Dad, Poor Dad* by Robert Kiyosaki

5. *Keys to Success 2.0* by Caleb Maddix

6. *How to Make Money as a Kid* by Caleb Maddix

7. *How to Have Unstoppable Confidence* by Caleb Maddix

8. *Think & Grow Rich* by Napoleon Hill

Each of these books taught me really good lessons about discipline, confidence, money, success, and working hard. Not only do I read books, I also listen to audiobooks a lot. This can be great for kids that really don't like to read. For me, my dad had me listen to audiobooks before I could even read so I started liking them at a young age.

To learn more, you need to:

1. Read Success Books - spend at least 30 minutes a day reading a success book or a book that is helping you learn more skills for your obsession.

2. Watch Videos - Instead of using YouTube for watching entertaining videos, spend time watching motivational and learning videos.

Make sure that you get your parent's permission first before you do this.

3. Listen to Audiobooks - If you don't really like to read, get audiobooks. You can still get the great information from the book, but these let you listen and take notes.

4. Listen to Podcasts - There are thousands of podcasts that cover so many things. You can listen to a podcast about sports, art, cooking, singing, education, etc. Try to find some podcasts that interest you and start listening to those.

5. Go to Live Events - A few years ago, my dad took me to a Grant Cardone event. It was

awesome! I was able to meet Grant Cardone and learn so much from the event.

At the event, I raised my hand to ask a question. I was called up on stage where Grant Cardone, Elena Cardone, Brad Lea, and Albert Preciado were answering questions from the audience. I asked Albert Preciado what are his three keys to success. He said to surround yourself with positive people who will encourage and support you. The second is to have courage and confidence in yourself. And finally, he said to find mentors that are mastering what you want to learn.

Willie Escobar, who also attended the event, told me that whenever you're sad or down, you need to focus on your dreams and not your past. He said that your dreams are bigger than anything you can think of. As you can see, live events allow you to meet other people that are trying to learn more, and you get great information.

I want to be honest. Learning is not always my favorite thing to do. I really like playing soccer and video games. Also, if I try to sit down and read, I can become distracted by the TV and my cell phone. To help me stay focused, my dad makes me read 30 minutes before I can play video games or get on my phone.

Learning is so important, but it can be easy to get distracted. Try to schedule your learning times. Find at least 30 minutes during the day to do some kind of learning. Choose from the list I provided and take notes. As Caleb Maddix says, "The person that is hungriest to learn will always be fed the most results." If you are hungry for knowledge, you will receive the greater amount of success.

Chapter 7
Take Action Now

It's great to learn new information and get excited about doing work, but until you actually take action, you haven't really done anything great. Action is so important. After you gain knowledge, it's time to start working hard. And the harder you work, the greater your results will be.

Let's say that you have two runners, Bob and Olivia. They each go for a run every single day. Bob runs 2 miles while Olivia runs 3. Even though Olivia is only running 1 more mile than Bob, she will get more results by pushing a little bit harder.

Kobe Bryant, one of the best basketball players of all time, woke up at 4:30 am everyday for practice while his teammates woke up at 7:30 am. That means that Kobe had 3 extra hours to practice. The extra action he took brought him the better results.

Grant Cardone says there are 4 degrees of action.

1. No action

2. Retreat (Go backwards, fear)

3. Normal Action

4. Massive Action

Massive Action is the level that you want to be on because that means that you are working harder than anyone else and receiving unbelievable results.

Becoming a success takes time, effort, and hard work. It will not happen overnight. It took Kobe Bryant years to become one of the best basketball players of all time. Lionel Messi, a professional soccer player, said, "It took me 17 years and 114 days to become an overnight success."

It's not going to just take you one day of taking action or two days, or three days. It is going to take massive action every single day. You must work hard and do your best to become better every day. No one is going to make your dream come true. You have to do it for yourself.

Don't just read this book and then put it back in the bookshelf. Read it, take notes, make a plan, and start taking action everyday. I'm trying to take action by learning, studying, growing, and listening to my mentors. I know that you are going to do the same because you were smart enough to get this book. Take the advice of an 8-year-old that is changing the world. Becoming successful is not easy. Average is easy, but savage can be hard. But once you break it down into the steps I provided in this book, it becomes easier. In fact, it's so simple, it's elementary!

Chapter 8
Create Your Own Future

The elementary entrepreneur is not just me, it's you too. It's everyone who wants to be savage. It's for kids that have been told they can't do it because they are too young. It's for kids who are having trouble in school but desire to have a savage future.

Make a commitment today and join the movement. I would love for you to send me a picture of your written goals and let me know what your thoughts are about this book. Please send me your response to www.theelementaryentreprenuer.com

I hear adults saying that technology is changing so fast. A long time ago people had to write a book by hand. Today there are voice recording apps that put your voice on paper and computers that made it easier for me to write this book.

Also, video online courses are a new way of learning. Videos are a great way to learn because you can watch it over and over again until you understand the message. Any kid can learn with videos no matter how young you are.

That is why I created a video course for kids who want to be elementary entrepreneurs. My goal is to impact millions of kids through a video course. My video course is designed to help kids be confident, teach them the benefits of having a great attitude, and learn the importance of sales and communicational skills while still being a kid.

You don't have to wait until you're 18 years old to make money or take massive action. If you want, you can even retire your parents or pay for your own college education. Age is just a number and you can do anything. If you can dream it, you can achieve it. It's ELEMENTARY! It's easy! All you need is desire, a mentor, and the ability to take massive action today and join the movement of elementary entrepreneurs who are changing the world one kid at a time.

Made in the USA
Columbia, SC
17 May 2018